Essays on Educational Reconstruction in India

Essays on Educational Reconstruction in India

BY

K. M. PANIKKAR, B.A. (Oxon)

GYAN

Published by

GYAN

Gyan Publishing House
5, Ansari Road
Daryaganj, New Delhi-110002
Phone: 011-47034999, 9811692060
E-mail: books@gyanbooks.com

Distribution Network
gyanbooks.com
India, USA, Canada, UK, Australia

ISBN: 978-81-212-8462-2 (HB)
First Published, 1920

2nd Impression 2024

Printed at: Gyan Press, Delhi.

ESSAYS ON EDUCATIONAL RECONSTRUCTION IN INDIA
Author: K. M. PANIKKAR

ESSAYS ON EDUCATIONAL RECONSTRUCTION IN INDIA

Essays on Educational Reconstruction in India

BY

K. M. PANIKKAR, B.A. (Oxon)

Sometime Dixon Research Scholar of
Christ Church, Oxford
Fellow of the Royal Anthropological Institute
Professor of History at M. A. O. College, Aligarh.

MADRAS

GANESH & CO.

1920

To

S. ROSS MASOOD

Director of Public Instruction

Hyderabad (Deccan)

CONTENTS

ESSAYS ON EDUCATIONAL RECONSTRUCTION IN INDIA

INTRODUCTION

THREE of the four Essays in this volume were written while the author was still at Oxford. Since that time he has been connected with one of the most important educational institutions in India which has brought him into close touch with the problems of Indian Education. He has also had opportunities of coming into close contact with the educational authorities of more than one important Indian state. These experiences have however only convinced him of the general soundness of the position he has taken up in these Essays.

The last two years in India have witnessed a

steady growth of opinion with regard to educational problems. The Calcutta University Commission, presided over by so eminent an educationist as Sir Michael Sadler and containing such distinguished men as Prof. Ramsay Muir, Sir Ashutosh Mukherjea and the Hon'ble Dr. Zia-ud-din Ahmad have issued a comprehensive report which though .concerned mainly with the Calcutta University deal with broad questions of educational principle, organisation and policy that it can be said to mark as definite step in the history of Indian education. The report of Prof. Patrick Geddes on "the proposed University for Central India, at Indore" and the Memorandum of Prof. P. Seshadri on "a University for Baroda" are also documents of importance in the growth of Indian educational opinion.

These are only reflective of the vast changes that have been taking place in India, movements that have been broadening the basis and renovating the ideals of Indian society. The last quarter of a century has brought nations and civilisations more into direct contact with one another. Englishmen have found out as Sir

Michael Sadler said lately that India is but next door. The reaction of this culture-contact has been tremendous in India. It is expressing itself in all phases of national life. In politics, in art, in literature, no less than in education, this movement to examine, to re-adjust and if necessary to reform has been very decided and clear.

The profound and far-reaching changes that have come over India during the last 15 years need not be elaborated here. The Indian Renascence of this century is certainly a fact comparable alike in its massive effect as in its varied forms to the great movement in Europe during the later half of the 15th century. A slow inward unrest preparing for great and fundamental social changes is the main characteristic of the Indian life of to-day.

The educational unrest is but a phase of this wider movement. The conviction has gained ground that the present system of education in India is thoroughly ineffective and does not in any way help in the great programme of reconstruction before us; that it is dogmatic in its character, restrictive in its operation, meaninglessly elaborate in its method and wasteful in its results; that in fact it is not animated by any high social ideals or principles of progress. It has become increasingly evident that if the programme of social reconstruction, by which alone India can take her place among the nations of the world, is to be realised, a sound system of national education Indian in its character and universal in its interests, is absolutely essential and must precede all other reform.

That the Anglo-Indian system of education, is inadequate to meet our expanding needs should not surprise us. The Indian University system arose out of the interested efforts of missionaries. A glance at the history of English education in India would prove the fact that neither the missionaries who actively endeavoured, nor the governmental authorities who supported them, were actuated by any altruistic desire to educate the Indian peoples in order to mould them into an Indian nation. The Rt. Hon'ble Charles Grant, the earliest advocate of English Education in India, in his "Enquiry into the measures which might be adopted by Great Britain for the improvement of the condition of her Asiatic subjects emphasises that English education would "silently under-mine and at length subvert the fabrick of error" ([1]) "undoubtedly, the most important communication the Hindus could receive" he says "would be the knowledge of our religion. . . . whereever this knowledge is received idolatory with all the rabble of its impure deities, its monsters of wood and stone, its false principles and corrupt practices, its delusive hopes and vain fears, its ridiculous ceremonies and degrading superstitions, its lying legends and fraudulent impositions would fall."([2]) The same idea underlies Macaulay's meaningless jokes at "seas of treacle and seas of butter" and at "astronomy which would move laughter in the girls at an English boarding school."

It is not suggested here that a deliberate policy of christianising India through education was followed by the Government. But it was hoped such

---

[1] "An enquiry into the measures" &c., by Charles Grant 1792, printed in Printed Parliamentary Papers (Indian) General App. I.

[2] Ibid.

results would follow. As the Missionaries were (and to a great extent still are) the chief agents of this system of Anglo-Indian education, they were no doubt justified in this attitude. The ideal of christianising India through education was from their point of view a noble and high ideal. That it was not successful is certainly due to no lack of effort on their part. It should not therefore be a matter of surprise to us that this education meant avowedly for the purpose of "subverting the fabrick of error" was found, when the time came, to be inadequate to the changing needs of society; "to be too soulless to be a living, energising method of building up the intellectual and moral life of the nation." (1)

The main defect of the present system of education is that its social ideals are entirely different from and to a very great extent hostile to Indian conditions. Institutional elements find no place in the studies promoted by our Universities. The social philosophy that is current in the colleges is not applied critically

---

[1] H. H. The Aga Khan. India in Transition p. 225, Lond. 1918.

and rationally to our institutional life and it gives to our education an air of unreality. Education given in the universities should bear some direct relation to our social life. This is possible only when it is recognised that education is but one aspect of national life and is itself only a means to fuller and greater development of the individual and his harmonisation with society. Criticism of societal traditions, and formulation of social ideals no less than free opportunity for the progressive variations of the individual and slow reconciliation of social conservatism with evolutionary principles, are therefore essentials of any national system of education. The Anglo-Indian system dominated as it was by the Missionaries, naturally and almost inevitably failed in this matter as the social ideal they formulated for India was revolutionary and involved a complete break from India's past traditions.

The other defects of the system, the undue importance attached to English as a course of study and as the medium of instruction, the formal and stereotyped methodology, the overwhelming emphasis on examination, all these have met with strong condemnation. India has realised that extensive reconstruction not merely of the superstructure but of the very ground work of our educational system is necessary for all progress.

But the problem is vast and varied. For one thing as Prof. Patrick Geddes[1] remarks "the present system of miseducation must continue until educational methods are renewed, indeed rediscovered, as they are being even by some of the present generation." The present Universities cannot all be replaced immediately and the process of striking out a sound and definite policy from amidst clashing opinion and opposing schools for so vast a country and heterogeneous a people would take time. We must however guard ourselves against any attempt at educational uniformity throughout India. There is wide room in India for a diversity of ideals, methods and institutions and we need not copy from any single European country, when the field is so wide and opportunities are so great. Let us have Universities and schools of all

---

[1] Prof. Patrick Geddes. University for C. I. P. 3.

types, the residential system of Oxford, the unicollegiate teaching system of America, the free, open, lecturing system of France and Switzerland. India is big enough for them all.

The educational unrest has however been confined to the university system and secondary education has so far been out of the range of public discussion. The questions of extension lectures, workmen's classes, rural schools are still unthought of by the Indian public. The truly stupendous and urgent problem of a special educational policy for the outcastes has also been ignored by the great majority of those who talk on education. The vital question of the education of women has been taken up both by the government and by the people but much remains to be done in this line also. The following Essays do not pretend to deal amply with these questions. Their purpose is a more modest one. They were written as studies on selected problems of Indian education in a spirit of constructive criticism from the point of view of Indian Nationalism.

The author wishes to express his thanks to the Rev. A. E. J. Rawlinson and Sir Roland Wilson

Bart. ([1]) both of whom read through the Essay 'On the problem of National Education'. He is also obliged to Mr. H. S. L. Polak for suggesting to him the desirability of studying the problem of "vernaculars as the media of instruction in secondary schools."

[1] Since the above was written the melancholy news of the death of Sir Roland Wilson at the age of 80 has reached me. His death creates an irreparable gap in the ranks of the too few Englishmen who were interested in the cultural side of Indian movements.

I

THE PROBLEM OF NATIONAL EDUCATION

"The questions of National Education, answer them as you will, touch the life and death of nations."

—LORD MORLEY.

I

THE PROBLEM OF NATIONAL EDUCATION

I

THOUGHT and word, it has been well said, are inchoate action; and every institution that considers its moral or legal right as an insufficient guarantee for its continued existence tries to control not only men's actions but their thoughts and words. Every government that is interested in maintaining the *status quo* thus finds itself invariably trying to mould the thoughts and opinions of men, not merely in those spheres that directly affect the governmental institutions but in all the varied phases of human activity. The best method of such a control has been at all times recognised to lie in the effective manipulation of the educational machinery of the community. The extreme re-

---

Read before the East India Association, London with Sir Roland Wilson (Bart) in the chair.

publicanism of the government of France is being imposed upon the community by its educational policy, just in the same way as the autocratic monarchy of Prussia tried to perpetuate itself by a State control of the universities.

This principle, which has been from time immemorial the mainstay of every party in power, is best illustrated by the educational policy of the British government in India. Indeed, education seems to have been at no time free and unhindered in our country. Brahminical India used all the power which it possessed in trying to impose a status education which would perpetuate its own supremacy. It is easy for a critic to find exact parallels for our present educational disabilities in the general policy of Brahminical India. If we now object that education is given to us through the medium of a foreign language, it could effectively be pointed out that Brahminical India did the same thing, insisted on education through Sanskrit, which being the language of the conquering Aryans, was a foreign language to the vast majority of the inhabitants of that time as English is to-day. If we now object that naval and military education is prohibited and opportunities for higher engineering and constructive skill are denied to us under the British government, it could be pointed out that the punishment for a Sudra *hearing* the sacred words of the Vedas was mutilation. And that at no time of Indian history were educational disabilities so wide, and so rigorously enforced as in Brahminical India.

Such an argument does our cause no harm. It only establishes beyond doubt our principle that the powers that be have always tried 'to continue to be' by an effective control of opinion through the educational machinery. In India under Britain, as in India under the Brahmins, the preservation of racial supremacy is the fundamental and apparently unalterable maxim of policy. This distrust of freedom is the basic fact that we have to face, and any reconstruction of Indian educational values must be preceded by a change in this essentially wrong attitude towards social growth.

Indian education is now wholly under the

control of the State. The State manages and moulds educational policy and ideal as thoroughly and as effectively as ever the Church or the Jesuits did. The universities are founded on government charter and exist on its sufferance. Their governing bodies are government-controlled. Their examinations are the only gateway to government appointment, thus discouraging all independent educational attempts. It inspects the curriculum, discourages the study of certain subjects, encourages the extensive diffusion of certain others, and tries to circumscribe the intellect in narrow grooves. It limits the activity of the teacher, prohibits him from having opinions on vital questions, imposes upon him obligations which no honourable and patriotic citizen could accept. The history of the educational policy in India is the history of the progressive systematisation of this distrust of freedom, of the progressive adoption of the principle of status education, of the progressive elaboration of the methodology to realise that principle.

The universal control of our educational institutions by the state is the most demoralising fact in the complicated problem of our national existence. Even such institutions as the Benares Hindu University, which comes into existence with the blessing of the Government, do not by any means escape this vigorous and all-embracing control of the Indian bureaucracy. It is suspected and watched. The Government reserves the right of disapproving the nomination of any professor. It refuses to sanction Hindi as the medium of education. When even such a conservative institution is under suspicion, it is impossible that independent experiments such as the Gurukula and the Santiniketan should be left alone. The Government is keeping a watchful eye on them and we may be certain that it would never allow those institutions in any way to interfere with its general policy of educational control.

This however is not the only defect of our educational policy. An education for the express purpose of maintaining status relations necessarily tends to become formal. Its methodology becomes rigid and loses its meaning. As it is animated by no principle of progression but only by a desire to better the machinery, its formalism comes to be of the most deadening type ensuring a 'Chinese' type of stationary society. Such a process is inevitable and the educational policy of the British Government since 1835 has shown this more conclusively than ever.

Macaulay wrote his omniscient minute in that year. It laid once and for ever the basis of the Anglo-Indian system of education. We are not concerned here with a criticism of that system; our business in this essay is to analyse and interpret a National educational ideal. What we have to recognise with regard to the Anglo-Indian system is that from 1834 its tendency has been to become progressively unreal, so that to-day it is a machinery which stunts our growth, a mass of unreality expressing no meaning and capable of expressing none, a system which tortures us by its elaboration, and kills our mind and soul by its barrenness.

Lord Curzon was the only Viceroy who came to India with any ideas on education. He recognised the mischief that had been done in the preceding 65 years and valiantly tried to reform it. In an address to the Educational

Conference at Simla he expressed in his own magniloquent style all the glaring defects of the Anglo-Indian system. He declaimed with vehemence against the 'attempt to transplant the smaller educational flora from the hot houses of Europe' into an entirely different atmosphere. The never-ending revolution of the examination wheel by which the educational fate of a man was settled met with the violent disapprobation of Lord Curzon. Indian education, he admitted, is restricted in its aims and destructive in its methods. 'It is of no use,' says he, 'to turn out respectable clerks, munsiffs or vakils if this is done at the expense of the intellect of the nation.'

Lord Curzon's criticism of the educational policy of the British Government was crushing and conclusive. But his reformative attempt, it must be admitted, ended in a total failure. His ideal was not free education, but an education, controlled by the State. The Apostle of Efficiency cannot tolerate a variety of institutions with different ideals and methods. They must needs be regulated by the State. The Universities already under Government influence must become directly Government controlled; otherwise they won't be efficient—as though efficiency were the end of educational institutions. The Raleigh Commission reported very much as Lord Curzon desired. In spite of the vigorous protest of Sir Gurudas Bannerjea, the Commission came to the conclusion that the cost of higher education should be raised and that a greater control of the university by the Government will tend to educational efficiency.

The Indian national movement had watched with great anxiety the restless activity of Lord Curzon in this field. The Congress awoke at last to the extreme importance of the problem when Lord Curzon showed them that the future of their country was being moulded by an Anglo-Indian Committee. Till now the Congress had shown a fatuous indifference to this supremely important subject. The pressing necessity of a national programme in education and the fatal danger of allowing an alien Government full control of the training of the youth of the nation, patent enough to ordinary observers of political life, were completely ignored by the Congress until this time. It is true that a few devoted spirits of the Congress movement had for a long time seen the imperative character of this problem. Surendra Nath Bannerjea, Gopal Krishna Gokhale, and a few others had very early in their career recognised the necessity of national control in education and had realised that the problem of national education touched very vitally the life and death of nations. They had in their different spheres tried to solve that problem independently of the Government. But the Congress itself confined its activities to the strictly political problems as if the source from which all political action derived its motive force was not a question of politics at all.

But the threatening activity of the Viceroy awoke the Congress from its characteristic slumber. The changed character of the Congress, its new and unbending nationalism, its gradual emancipation from the Bombay clique, all contributed to the general activity and life which that movement showed during the latter part of the Curzonian regime. Lord Curzon's attempt to raise the cost of higher education was therefore met with a direct challenge. The Congress at

Benares enunciated the formula of 'National Education under National Control.' Later events showed that this formula was interpreted in two entirely different ways by the two different parties. The vital difference between the two parties showed itself even in the interpretation of this non-political programme. To the Moderates of the Gokhale type national education and national control meant only an extension of the field for Indians in the Service and a greater study of Indian subjects in the universities. To the Nationalists this formula meant something very different. They interpreted it to mean the complete nationalisation of educational machinery and absolute boycott of all the institutions where the hand of the Government was suspected. Thus the Congress committed itself to an undefined formula which only covered, as all formulae are perhaps meant to cover, fundamental differences of opinion. Behind the united demand for national education under national control which the Congress put forward in 1905, it was easy for the acute observer to see the uncompromising hostility betwen the Moderates and the Nationalists.

The cleavage of opinion on the matter became vital when from the domain of congressional discussion an attempt was made to translate it into the field of action. Bengal instituted a Council of National Education and it seemed for a time that the educational monopoly of the Government was passing out of its hands. But the Bengal attempt failed as it was bound to fail. A division between the purse and the brain of a concern cannot indeed conduce to its success. The Hindu revival which was at the basis of the new nationalist movement had scarcely affected the moderates. They were still the 'crowning product of the British rule,' as one of them expressed it. They still looked to England for inspiration. They were unwilling to nationalise education completely lest 'the crowning product of the British rule' might become extinct. The Nationalist party had no such fears. They looked not to Europe but to India itself for inspiration. To them, all the faith of the moderates in the wonderful effects of the western education was but one of the many vile superstitions which the Anglo-Indian system had sedulously cultivated. As the experiment of national education progressed, this divergence of opinion came more and more to the front. In a few years' time the whole system had completely broken down. Few tears need be wasted on the failure of this scheme. It only emphasised once more the fundamental political truth that all great institutions that shape and mould the destiny of nations begin in individuals, and not in collective organised groups. The great pre-revolutionary educational force in Europe was the Society of Jesus and it had its origin in the brain of Ignatius Loyola. Comenius, Pestallozi and Froebel and all the rest of the great teachers that have revolutionised the educational systems of the world and thus directed the thought and evolution of mankind into widely different moulds were individuals and the institutions that they set up did not owe their origin to the collective initiation of a group but to individual attempts to realise what society had generally laughed at as impracticable dreams. In this matter as in others real progress can come only by the action of individuals and the Bengal National Council of Education had this 'basic fault.' It was left for an individual, the most eminent that Bengal has produced after Chaitanya, to realise the ideal of National Education and Rabindranath Tagore's school at Bolpur can in this way be said to be the contribution of Bengal to the solution of this problem. We shall examine it later.

The Bengal Council was perhaps the most typical attempt of modern Anglicised and 'progressive' India in the educational field. But the most remarkable experiment both in educational ideal and pedagogic methodology came not from Bengal but from the Punjab. The Arya Samaj and the Hindu revival brought with them not only a new interpretation of the doctrines of the Aryan religion but also a new outlook on life, and a new conception of mental training. The Aryas recognised more fully than the Congressionists that the development of an independent system of education must precede all attempts at reconstruction and readjustment of the bases of Indian society. This new attitude and outlook materialised in the Gurukula at Hardwar.

The Gurukula ideal of education is essentially different, not only from the Anglo-Indian system but from the educational ideals of any of the modern countries. It is an attempt to revitalise the ascetic spirit of the ancient Hindu Culture. It is an experiment in assimilating as much of modern science as is essential with the spirit of our ancient civilisation. The Gurukula tries to found an Indian University, Indian in every sense, out of which would arise a new Indian nation breathing the old and sacred atmosphere of the Vedas but tasting and relishing all that is useful and fine in the thought, literature and science of the modern nations.

This is, we might say at once, the right ideal. But in the systematic elaboration of its methodology the Gurukula system tends both to an ascetic severity, and a cast-iron formalism. In taking the children away from the realities of domestic life and interning them for very nearly 18 years in the unreal surrounding of a Himalayan monastery, the Arya Samaj theorists show an absolute ignorance of the fundamental ideas of education. They forget the essential truth that an education which does not keep the child in touch with the realities of domestic life is no education at all; that to be left after 20 years of restless mental activity in an unexplained and to him inexplicable environment is not only harmful but positively destructive; that such a divorce of life in knowledge and life in reality can only lead to intellectual insincerity absolutely incompatible with true education.

The answer which the Aryasamajists make to this argument is that family influence in India is on the whole detrimental to the full development of the child and that the less he sees of his family in his formative years the better. This line of argument takes for granted that it is for his elders to settle what is good for the child, and in effect that the mind of the child is soft clay to be moulded and shaped as his elders desire. This is the doctrine against which the great Comenius and the no less great Rousseau preached with such unanswerable logic. The child's mind is not a virgin soil to use the famous metaphor of Comenius, to be sown by the teacher in a formal pattern.

This is the basic flaw of the Gurukula system. It treats the children as so much raw material to be manufactured by a longtime process into pious, patriotic, philosophical and literary citizens capable of carrying the Message of the Great Arya Civilisation to all the known parts of the world.

Another and perhaps more effective criticism on the Hardwar ideal is that it is essentially revivalistic and therefore lacking in the element of progression. The ideals of yesterday are useless if they are not interpreted from the point of view of the life of to-day. The *Gurukulas* were prevalent full 2000 years ago and it is a vain attempt even if it were possible to revitalise an institution which flourished under widely different conditions and in a very different time. No nation can go back and least of all could we who boast of having had a continuous civilised existence of 4000 years, afford to go back to a particular phase of our national evolution. Societal traditions have their place in educational systems and in India, or at least in the India of the Indians, such traditions are stronger than even a traditionalist could wish. Every system of education should have both the binding conservatism of the social tradition and the fluidal mobility of a progressional element. The former is the hold of the past. The latter is the problem of the present and the call of the future. In Indian institutions the former is predominant; the latter is deplorably lacking. The Gurukula of Hardwar shows this defect of our institutions more conspicuously than anything in modern India.

The principle of individual freedom so crushed out in Hardwar for uniformity of pattern is found to be the fundamental principle of the *Santiniketan* of Rabindranath Tagore. The Bengal Council was not an educational experiment; it was a solemn futility meant to be an educational demonstration. But that unrest which drove the fatuous Congress to do something in its own extremely futile manner led the most fertile mind of modern Bengal to embark on an educational experiment the most unique of its kind in India. The School at Bolpur showed once more that experiment must begin, especially when the raw material on which it is begun is the most precious element in the nation, with the tested instincts of creative genius, and not by the commercial application of a uniform principle. The Santiniketan grew out of Tagore's brains as the Academy grew out of Plato's and the Bonnal School out of Pestalozzi's dreams.

Educational practice has from time immemorial been divided, as one writer well put it, into that which works through rules more than through sympathy and that which puts sympathy before rule. The Hardwar system exemplifies the first: the Bolpur system exemplifies the second. The Hardwar system works through the class, assumes a uniformity of intelligence and interest. Santiniketan works through the individual, treats 'each case on its own merit' with no uniformity of pattern and preconceived notions as to what the child ought to be when grown up. It assumes that every child is born good but with different degrees of instinct, feeling and intelligence. The aim of all is the same but the capability of realising it differs in degree. Thus each individual should be ministered to in the fashion that fits him and brings out and developes his qualities and not in the measure of another's wants and desires.

The teaching of tradition tends to societal control: individual liberty tends to social freedom; but societal control and individual freedom are not incompatible when we recognise that, individual liberty finds its highest and truest expression only under societal control. But though they are not necessarily incompatible popular instinct is right when it draws a dividing line between the rigid formalism of the traditionalist and the sympathetic guidance of the individualist. The Gurukula stands for the control and therefore for the limitation of the future by the experience or the realised ideal of the past. Bolpur stands for the ideal of free development deriving inspiration from tradition, but hindered as little as possible by the deadweight of a desire to bring back into existence an institution out of which life had flown centuries ago.

Both the Gurukula and the Santiniketan are only individual attempts at the solution of a national problem. Realisation of great principles can only come through the spontaneous energy of individuals: but institutions meant for remedying crying evils have to originate, not in the creative genius of a single man, but in the general consciousness of a nation and its collective initiative. The Benares Hindu University is essentially a work of this kind. It is not the realisation of a great principle or ideal but simply an attempt to remedy the most conspicuous of all the evils of the Anglo-Indian system of education. Macaulay had written with the sublime impudence that characterised his peculiar talents that the Indian *risorgimento* can come only through the wide diffusion of European culture and that Indian civilisation, whatever it may have been worth, was as dead as the Assyrian. The falsity of this view was manifest from its beginning. Its importance lies in its results rather than on its merits. From that day dates the deplorable divorce of Indian education from Indian thought and Indian feeling. The universities of India were but factories where a few were manufactured into Graduates and a good many more wrecked in the voyage of their intellectual life.

What the Hindu University has attempted to do is to bring Indian education into conformity with Indian culture. With its many and patent faults we need not concern ourselves. What we should recognise clearly is that the Hindu University differs essentially from the Anglo-Indian Universities in that the former exists for the express purpose of interpreting Hindu culture, and as the material and tangible expression of the cultural unity of India. Thus the Benares University is a far-reaching experiment remedial in its primary character but creating a new atmosphere, vitalising old traditions, interpreting racial ideals and spreading the thought and feeling of ancient and modern India.

Here we have the right ideal. But in the execution of that ideal lies unsolved the problem of national education. The Benares University is as effectively controlled by the Government as its own institutions. The experiment is so important, the probable effects from it so far-reaching, the success or failure of it so vital, that the Government acting on this irrational distrust of free and unshackled education considered itself justified in imposing its own authority on it. But when all is said of the influence of Government, of the reactionary character of any institution that exists to interpret ancient ideals and not primarily to search for truth, of the mischief that it may originate due to its sectarian character, of the great and crying evils such as the caste system which it may perpetuate, when all is said, the Benares Hindu University remains a capital fact which is bound to influence our national evolution certainly in a much better way than the Anglo-Indian institutions.

Its chief defect we have noticed before. It is remedial and therefore supplementary. It does not solve the educational problem of nationalist India. It does not even face the issue boldly. But this must be admitted that it is a great step forward. It is the natural nucleus of any national experiment in education. Around it would gather institutions united in their diversity, inspired by the majestic flow of the sacred Ganges which now as before is held sacred by the great majority of Indian Population.

II

Up to now our work has been entirely critical and estimative. The greater task of stating and analysing the problem and interpreting the tendency of the new nationalists towards it remains.

What most strikes anyone who approaches the problem of Indian Education from any point of view, is its appalling magnitude. Here is a country with a population of 315 millions whose future salvation depends greatly upon the careful study and the right solution of this problem. Here is a not inconsiderable portion of the human kind whose destiny depends a great deal upon those who have the foresight to see and the energy and the enthusiasm to realise a right educational ideal. The problem is indeed bewildering in its variety. It is as if one entered a primeval forest, thick and crowded with trees, with no gleam of light to guide one's steps, with soft grass and wild creepers covering many a pitfall. But if it is difficult, nay almost impossible to traverse, we must also admit the temptation to persevere in the attempt is as great, seeing that beyond this dark and untraversed forest lies the promised land, the land of a free and educated population.

Out of the wild variety of this problem three factors stand out towering above the rest. They are the questions of a common language, of the education of women, and of the general policy and the institutions by which to realise it. The first question is whether India should be treated as a cultural unity, whether a new All-Indian language, a modified *Arya Bhasha* embodying not only the culture of Ancient India, but assimilating the contribution of the Mussalman inhabitants should be consciously evolved. The second question is whether we should perpetuate the status relation between men and women in education, whether an absolute equality of sexes in educational practice is not bound to affect adversely the free progress of family and social development. Whether a different educational ideal for women is not desirable, possible and practicable. The third question is the question of the educational principles and institutions; whether a uniform general policy is desirable, if desirable how far it should be carried, whether the realisations of great principles does not come from the co-ordination of tested units, whether it would be more desirable to nationalise interest than to universalise it. Such are the main outlines of the problem which the nationalist has to face not only when India governs herself but even to-day, because without at least a partial solution of the educational problem Swaraj would remain an unrealised ideal.

The first question–that of a common language, is one of the most pressing of our problems not only from an educational, but from a general nationalist point of view. Without it all our efforts at united action must for ever remain virtually ineffective. It is true that before the British dominion India was one in feeling, thought and culture. But to-day by the influence of a foreign language her different provinces are tending to a difference even in these vital points. This process of disintegration can be arrested only by a common language. Is such a thing possible; if possible, can Indian Nationalists unaided by the all-pervading machinery of government realise it? This is the first question we have to answer.

That English can never serve the purpose of

a common language is a manifest fact that requires no argument to prove. It is so utterly foreign to us that education in it involves an enormous waste of mental power. This waste is suffered not only by those whose natural gifts are so overflowing as to be indifferent to its effects but by everyone who desires to be educated in India. This is the explanation of the enormous number of failures in our universities, and of that unique and therefore all the more heartrending phenomenon of the Indian educational world the "failed B.A." English can never become anything but the language for a microscopic minority of our inhabitants—the *cidevant* Eurasian. For us Indians it is and it will ever be a language in which to commit literary suicide, a tongue which stifles our expressive faculties, a medium of expression which kills all the thinking power of our mind. The use of a foreign language as the medium of our higher education leaves us without a national genius in literature, in sciences and in thought. Lord Curzon was essentially right, though in a negative sense, when he said that the raising of the cost of higher education would tend to the betterment of India. Such an administrative act would limit the classes who would be affected by this intellectual ravage. It would confine the intellectual exploitation to the very few who are rich. The ordinary man, though he does not gain, surely does not lose by this arrangement.

Setting aside therefore the impossible supposition that English can at any time be the common language of India we are left with two alternatives, to wit:—that we should choose as our common language either an unused language—a dead language as it is erroneously called—Sanskrit, Prakrit, or Classical Persian, or, one of the chief Indian vernaculars, such as Hindi, Bengali or Tamil. Of these two possible alternatives we can dismiss the first with a few words. True that Sanskrit has the merit of being known and studied all over India. It has also the merit of being the common basis of all the Indian languages. But at *no time* does it seem to have been extensively spoken in India and it is hardly possible that such a perfect language with all its different verbal forms could ever be spoken by the ordinary man. Persian, of course, has little claim to be the common language, and Prakrit, less.

Thus we are left with indubitable fact that the common language of India can only be one of the three or four chief vernaculars of India. The problem more plainly stated becomes this: which language are we to choose, from among the great vernaculars of India as the medium of higher education and the basis of higher communal life? The apparent contest is between Hindustani,[1] Bengali and Tamil. But the contest seems to me to be only an apparent one. Neither Tamil nor Bengali, however cultivated their literatures be, can claim to be anything but the language of a particular province, a language spoken by a sub-nationality. But the case of Hindustani is different. The Hindustani-speaking people do not inhabit a particular marked out

---

[1] I use the word Hindustani in the sense which Gierson has given to it *i.e.*, the language which the ordinary man speaks in Northern India, of which both Urdu and Hindi are mere literary offshoots. I am convinced that the bad feeling that existed between the two communities with regard to Urdu and Hindi does not affect our argument in favour of *Hindustani.*

portion of India. It is in fact understood all over North India. It is understood in a slightly different form by all the Mussalman inhabitants of India and this fact alone makes its claim a matter of incontestable weight. Also it has a double alphabet which, peculiarly enough, is in this case not a hindrance but an additional claim. Its Nagari character makes it acceptable to all Hindus; its Urdu character makes it acceptable to all Mussalmans. Thus an acceptance of Hindustani would preserve the continuity of our civilisation both for our Muslim brethren and for ourselves.

It is an interesting and supremely important subject which we would have liked to discuss with greater elaboration had the limits of this essay permitted it. However before entering into the consideration of the next question we would attempt to answer one important objection that is commonly raised against the evolution of an Indian common language. Will not the adoption of any one Indian language, say Hindustani for example, as our *lingua franca* adversely affect the growth of our vernaculars? Will not the language in which Chandidas and

Rabindranath Tagore wrote, say these, become in course of time, like Gaelic in Ireland, merely a dead tradition. Will not the sublime Tirukural, and the no less sublime Songs of Ramdas, become like the wonderful poems of the Welsh bards, or the reputed epics of the Aztecs, mere object of curiosity for the antiquarians? The fear is legitimate, though groundless. The unique greatness of India lies in its wonderful diversity, and the ideal of a great India must always remain a diversity-ideal. Is the attempt to create a common language an attempt to create a uniformity of thought and expression? If it is, it is treason to India. But under no conceivable circumstances can it be so. A second language taught and spoken as such can never replace a well cultivated mother tongue. The Bengali would be proud of his tongue as the Tamilian, the Gujerati, the Punjabi and the Malayali would be. They would be cultivated with greater zest and interest as the knowledge of the other Indian languages grew among the people. The objection therefore is groundless.

The proper education of women is the next problem. We have noticed that this problem has to be treated in three main lines, which are —first, whether we should perpetuate the status relation between men and women in education, secondly, whether the Indian family life does not demand a peculiar consideration in our educational problem, thirdly, whether a different educational ideal for our women cannot without breaking the continuity of our culture be evolved from our past.

The Indian nation can never be free till the Indian woman has ceased to be a slave. The Indian nation can never be educated till the Indian woman has ceased to be ignorant. I am not saying that the Indian womanhood is bound in slavery, or that it is blinded by ignorance. But the fact is that both in the relative status of sexes and in the idea of their education our present system affords room for very considerable modification. Is that modification to come through the activities of the social reformers or by the extensive diffusion of education. The difference between the two processes is great indeed. The social reformers try to impose their ideas on the generality, believing implicity in the infallibility of the reforms they advocate. The social reform temperament is the temperament of the missionary. On the other hand the process of social evolution through the wider diffusion of education is essentially a process of raising the general standard of opinion and thus making social reform the real expression of the conscious will of the community.

The question however arises whether we are to perpetuate the status relation of sexes in our educational system. The process of human evolution has surely been in the progressive differentiation of sexes which has now become a dominant and capital fact in all organised societies. The question of sexual status and education affects us in an entirely different way. At present the education of our females, such as it is, is entirely in relation to the family and not to the community. It is designed so as to make the child as it grows up a sweet and docile wife, an ideal mother, and when she reaches that age a self-sacrificing widow and able head of the family. This ideal is absolutely right as far as it goes. But it does not go far. It gives no place for the relation of women to the community. That relation is only implied in a very limited sense in the ideal mother. The business of the mother, as far as the community is concerned, according to this ideal, is to rear up ideal citizens. Naturally the question arises: does the social relationship of women end with rearing up excellent soldiers and sagacious politicians? Is she merely a means and not an end in herself? Can her faculties be fully and freely developed except in relation to the organised community, and, by limiting her to the smallest possible community, the family, are we not limiting the development of her faculties? It is therefore evident that any comprehensive solution of the educational problem must include the final destruction of the artificial limitation of feminine relationship to the family.

This brings us to the second question whether such an extension of feminine activity through a different ideal of education which, while perpetuating the healthy status relation of sexes, does not limit the female to the family, would affect adversely that vital point of our civilisation—the joint family system. It is by no means clear whether a higher individuation of the units that compose the family would tend to its breakup and it does not seem to be true that a freer interpretation of the position of women in society must lead to a disintegration of the family. What seems quite clear is that the joint family system as it is, with all its merits, tends very considerably to be a dead-weight in the matter of freer, fuller and healthier family life, and a purification of it in its essentials can come only through the increased intelligence of women. Female education as long as it is imparted with the view of perpetuating the status relation of the sexes or on the other hand is based on the idea that such differences ought not to exist, would remain wholly unreal, disturbing the whole fabric of social organisation and sapping the very vital roots of all social existence. The education of women, such as is given in India to-day, inclines to the second alternative of ignoring the existence of sexual differences. That is why female education in India has been a totally disturbing, instead of a consolidating, factor in social life. The Indian joint family life being indeed the realised truth of a thousand generations requires a peculiar consideration in our educational problem. Our ideal should not be to destroy but to purify it.

Does this ideal mean a break in the continuity of our civilisation? In spite of the opinion of Sir C. Sankaran Nair, no sensible man has ever believed that according to Hindu ideals woman is created to minister to man's wants. The Hindu ideal of womanhood has been the ideal—not the European conception of a helpmate for man soothing his distracted hours—of a necessary counterpart without whom man by himself cannot attain salvation. What Sri Krishna asks his old playmate Kuchela when that pious devotee visited the Lord, is whether the female rishi suited him in every way. Indeed, according to the Hindu ideal man and woman are like the twin blade of a pair of scissors each impotent and insufficient in itself and capable of action only in combination. There is no superiority or inferiority in their relations. The right ideal is to make both the blades as keen as possible. This not only does not mean a break in the continuity of the Hindu tradition but is in entire conformity with its spirit. Such is the opinion of those who have devoted their life work to the cause of female education. Prof. Karve in founding the women's university has the same ideal. The Gurukula authorities in establishing an institution for girls gives the authority of orthodox Hinduism to this ideal.

Now it remains to discuss whether a general educational programme under these conditions is possible, and whether such a policy would be desirable as laying down the main lines of our educational development. A general policy means at least an attempt on the part of the powers that be to lay down certain things as the essential minimum of education. This power in the hands of a government generally tends to a control of the educational system. That is eminently undesirable, even if it comes from a strictly nationalist Indian Government. Education, unless we want to travesty it as a governmental instrument, must necessarily be free and unhampered. Thus a general policy can be laid down only to this extent, that is, the Government while encouraging, by every means in its power, should leave education outside the scope of its general activities except in so far as to remedy such manifest evils as a monopoly by any particular community, or a general inactivity in any particular field. The Government should make primary education free and compulsory, but in no case should it insist on a general curriculum for the whole of India. It should be left to the discrimination of the local authorities prescribing however that in such subjects, as elementary Arithmetic of which the realised experiments of the past centuries have convincingly proved the utility, a minimum standard should be set. Only up to this has the Government any right of interference. In its educational policy the Government's activity should be one of co-ordination of educational institutions.

How then are we to realise this ideal of free and compulsory primary education, absolutely under local control, with the least possible interference from the governmental authorities? Is it by a system of free universities as in America or by a system of local effort supplemented by board schools as in England? The answer is difficult. But this much we can say without any fear of contradiction: A national programme of education in a country like India whose greatness lies in the rich diversity of her people, her ideas and her life, must essentially be a programme of local effort, of individual experiment and of provincial and national co-ordination. The Government can therefore never lay down an educational policy. If it did, such a policy would only create a mechanical process of instruction without any local colour, without any conformity with the realities of life, without any attempt to create intellectual sincerity. The realisation of any ideal, however good, can come only through the general prevalence of individual experiments in that direction. A state can never successfully impose it on the community, without transforming the character of that ideal.

To summarise what we have said till now. The nationalist movement in India is threatened to-day by a grave danger, that of an inquisitorial control by the state of the educational machinery. On the face of it, therefore, a nationalist programme in education becomes an imperative necessity. From the earliest days of the national movement the more far-sighted among them had seen this. But their efforts remained mainly local until the hand of Lord Curzon imposed on an unwilling Congress the necessity of enunciating a general policy in education. The translation of that policy from the realm of speech to that of action ended in complete failure. But other experiments, such as the Gurukula which attempts to revive the ascetic spirit of the ancient Hindus and the Santiniketan which tries to realise the principle of individual freedom, arose out of that educational unrest. The Benares University expressed in a tangible form the dissatisfaction of the best moderate mind with the Anglo-Indian system of education.

But a really nationalist ideal in education has not yet been authoritatively elaborated. Such an ideal must take into consideration the problem of a common language, which in the opinion of the present writer can only be Hindustani. It must also give particular attention to the education of our women without attempting to disintegrate the joint family system. Finally a national educational programme must be a programme of local effort and national co-ordination. It is unnecessary to forecast whether such an ideal is immediately practicable. Any diversity-ideal can only be a matter of growth though not necessarily slow. The nationalist effort in education, therefore, should be directed not chiefly towards any attempt to mould the governmental policy but in building up local institutions of a great variety of character and embodying different national ideals and culture. Therein alone lies the hope of nationalism, for nationalism ignorant is nationalism ineffective.

Let us remember this and then we shall have no more fear of the future. In the past India was great : the present is not without hope : but with our united effort her future shall indeed be greater than either her present or even past. It depends upon us and let it not be said of us that the Spirit of Time in determining the fate of our Motherland tried us in the ordeal of fire and found us wanting.

II

VERNACULARS AS MEDIA OF INSTRUCTION IN SECONDARY SCHOOLS.

"A University which ignores the masses and contents itself with producing a few people possessing a high command of English must be pronounced to be a perversion of a University."

—C. R. REDDY.

"While I do not minimise the importance of education being given to a higher standard in the English language, I most emphatically maintain that for the sake of our nationality, our country and our religion it is even more necessary for education to be given in a thorough manner in the vernaculars."

—H. H. THE MAHARAJAH OF ALWAR.

II

VERNACULARS AS MEDIA OF INSTRUCTION IN SECONDARY SCHOOLS

NO problem has been so much debated in the Indian Educational World as the desirability of imparting education through the vernaculars. The opinion has steadily been gaining ground that the great and fundamental mistake in the current educational system of India is the use of English as the medium of instruction. An influential school of educationists, consisting of almost all the younger men trained in English Universities, has accepted that as the first principle of their activities. A no less influential school of politicians, again of the younger generation, has begun to echo the sentiment on popular platforms. It is therefore a matter deserving the greatest attention and my attempt here is merely to examine its influence on the system of secondary education in India.

To understand this problem fully it is necessary for us to review in outline the main facts concerning the growth of the present system. It is well known that the first educational activities of the company were mainly directed to the promotion of Brahminical and Islamic learning. ([1]) The enthusiasm of Warren Hastings ([2]) for Indian culture which manifested itself in his encouragement of monumental labours of Sir William Jones found tangible expression in the establishment of a Sanskrit College at Benares and a Madrassah at Calcutta. But his policy had its opponents even then. The Right Honourable Charles Grant as early as 1773 pleaded for educating the 'natives in English.' Later on in India itself Rammohun Roy, Hare and others were advocates of introducing English Education. They found support in Mr. Francis Warden, member of council, Bombay, who wrote in 1828 that "the study of *English*

---

[1] Vide Syed Mahmood : History of English Education in India.

[2] It is not so widely known as it deserves to be that Hastings wrote a very appreciative introduction to the *Gita*.

language should be made the primary and not the secondary object of attention in the education of the Native!"[1]

The question was for the time set at rest by the minute of Lord Macaulay, [2] dated the 2nd of Feb. 1835. His main arguments are well known. He put his weight definitely on the side of education of Indians through the medium of English hoping thereby that the seas of treacle and seas of butter would soon evaporate under the heat of European culture. In fact one of the main objects of the introduction of English as the medium of instruction and the English language as the chief subject of study was to undermine gradually, and if possible to subvert eventually, the religions and civilisation of India.

The Resolution of Lord William Bentinck's Government dated the 7th of March 1835 declared that "his Lordship in Council is of opinion that the great object of the British Government

[1] Quoted in Syed Mahmood's English Education in India. See *appendix*.

[2] Trevelyan on the education of the peoples of India.

is the promotion of European literature and science amongst the Natives of India and that all the funds appropriated for the purpose of education would be best employed on English education alone." Thus was taken what everybody admits to be the most momentous step in Indian education. English was made the sole channel of instruction. The encouragement given to oriental learning was stopped on the ground that "the money spent on the Arabic and "Sanskrit Colleges was not merely a dead loss to "the cause of truth; it was bounty money paid "to raise up champions of error and call into "being an oriental interest which was bound by "the conditions of its existence to stand in the "front of the battle against the progress of "European literature." ([1])

The unwisdom of the step that the Government took in making English the sole medium of instruction was even at that time realised by scholars and thinkers who were in touch with Indian opinion. H. H. Wilson, the great orien-

---

[1] *Trevelyan* on the Education of the people of India, pp. 87-91.

talist, in his history of British India (1848) pointed out that in this decision the Government had committed itself to a policy in which the interests of the great body of people were overlooked. "The great truth was also overlooked," he wrote, "that a national literature can only co-exist "with a national language and that as long as "knowledge is restricted to a foreign garb it "can be the property only of the few who can "command leisure and opportunity for its "attainment. It is obvious that a language "so utterly discordant with every Indian dialect "can never become the universal medium of "instruction; and that even if it should be "extensively studied it would constitute the "literature of a class and never that of a "people."

The injustice of the decision taken by the Government was soon recognised at least in theory. In their first annual report after 1835 the committee of public instruction declared that they were "deeply sensible of the importance of encouraging the cultivation of the vernacular languages." They added, "we conceive "the formation of a vernacular literature to be "the ultimate object to which all our efforts "must be directed. AT PRESENT the extensive "cultivation of some foreign language is ren-"dered indispensable by the almost total absence "of a vernacular literature and the consequent "impossibility of obtaining a tolerable education from that source only."

This ultimate object was steadily kept in view by the Government in India. And in the famous Dispatch of 1854 Sir Charles Wood as President of the Board of Control gave classic expression to the policy of concurrent development of vernacular literature and English education. He said: "it is neither our aim nor our desire to substitute the English language for the vernacular dialects of the country. We have always been most sensible of the importance of the use of the languages which alone are understood by the great mass of the population . . . . . It is indispensable therefore that in any general system of education the study of them should be assiduously attended to and any acquaintance with improved European knowledge which is to be communicated to the great mass of people can only be conveyed to them through one or other of those vernacular languages." He went on to add that the teaching of the English language should be combined with a careful attention to the study of the vernacular language and with such general instruction as can be conveyed through that language. "*We look therefore to the English language and the vernacular languages of India* TOGETHER *as the media for the diffusion of European knowledge* and it is our desire to see them cultivated together."

The excellent and unexceptionable policy of this Dispatch was however never given a chance. With the establishment of English universities in India and the consequent subordination of the interest of secondary education to the interests of the Universities a new policy of retrogression in secondary education gradually took the place of the generous and liberal ideas of the Dispatch of 1854. The High schools came to be entirely dependent upon the Universities and their influence has been by no means beneficial. Since the education given by the new Universities was entirely through English and consisted mainly in the study of

English subjects, the High schools which came to be dependent on them found it necessary to give less and less importance to the vernacular. English gradually monopolised the place which the Dispatch of 1854 had proposed it should divide with the vernacular. How quick this reaction was is seen from the following fact. The first regulation of the entrance examination to the Calcutta University allowed students to write their answers in *any living language.* The idea was that English should be taught in schools only as a language and should not take the place of the vernacular as the medium of instruction. But the domination of the University over secondary education, a matter seldom advantageous and never desirable, asserted itself and in 1861 it was ruled that all answers were to be given in English except when otherwise specified.

This was the beginning of that educational policy which has made secondary education in India one of the most inefficient, and without doubt the most wasteful, educational system in the world. Secondary education came to be moulded to the needs of English teaching universities and the interest of the great majority of students was sacrificed to the interest of the few who could afford, and to the still more few who could profit by, a college education.

The one important result of the regulation of 1861 in Calcutta (and similar regulations in the other university centres) was that English came to be the medium of instruction even in the very lowest classes. The effect of this departure manifested itself in two ways. First, in the utter neglect of the vernaculars and secondly in the great wastage of mental energy. The Commission of 1882 over which Sir William Hunter, the historian, presided and of which Kashi Nath Trimbak Telang was a member, recommended after considerable enquiry that in the middle school classes at least the vernacular should be used as the medium. They did not make any suggestion with regard to High schools. In Madras, the writer can remember that so late as 1904 and 5, when he was in the middle school classes, English was being used as the sole medium of instruction. He distinctly remembers being taught geography in the first form through English and History in the second form through the same language. School teachers had come to the conclusion that as English was to be the language in which answers were to be written in the matriculation examination, the sooner the student learnt it the better.

The disastrous results of this system were recognised by the Commission of 1902. They wrote: "Boys begin to learn English as a language, and also to learn other subjects through the medium of English long before they are capable of understanding it. We therefore venture to express our opinion that it is desirable that the study of English should not be permitted to begin till a boy can be expected to understand what he is being taught in that language." On this recommendation the Government of Lord Curzon issued a resolution which deplored that the cultivation of the vernaculars had been neglected "with the result that the hope expressed in the Dispatch of 1854 is as far as ever from realisation." The Government solemnly asserted "that it has never been part of our policy to substitute the English language for the vernacular dialects of the country."

They laid down that "a child should not be allowed to learn English as a language until it has made some progress in the primary stages of instruction and has received a thorough ground in his mother tongue; and that it is equally important that when the teaching of English has begun it should not be prematurely employed as the medium of instruction in other subjects."

Since that time the question has loomed large before the Indian public. Motions have been introduced into Legislative Councils, Imperial and Provincial, demanding the introduction of vernaculars as the media in schools. In the educational world also the question has been discussed to some extent and the Government of His Exalted Highness the Nizam has given a decisive answer by the establishment of the Osmania University, in which the sole language of instruction is *Urdu*. States like Travancore have encouraged the growth of an independent system of vernacular education with distinct success. And the Calcutta University Commission has made an elaborate and systematic enquiry into the whole problem.

Now, the short sketch of Indian Educational history in so far as it affects the problem before us, shows one thing definitely; and that is, that in spite of the most unexceptionable ideals enunciated from time to time in the Resolutions of governments, Central and Local, and despite the recommendations of Commissions consisting of eminent educational experts, secondary education has been carried on exclusively through the medium of English much to the detriment both of teachers and of students. For the short period of 7 years from (1854-1861) when the present educational system was just beginning to develop, an attempt was made for simultaneous advance. But under the influence of the new Universities the secondary schools soon adapted themselves to changed ideals with results so deplorable that the Government of India Resolution fifty years after the great Dispatch declared that the hope expressed then was as far as ever from realisation.

The question, it will now be recognised, is not one of recent origin. It is the fashion among certain people to stigmatise the movement for the supersession of English in schools as being engineered by those nationalists whose attitude towards the Government is of a doubtful character. It will not be doubted now that the movement started with the Court of Directors and the Government of India have repeatedly declared their sympathy with it. In view of this, the opposition from a section of the Indian public would have been inexplicable were it not known that a good many among the older generation of Indians have completely fallen under the spell of English, as a language.

About the effects of the use of English as the medium of instruction *in the schools* the evidence collected by the Sadler Commission is conclusive and convincing. Mr. F. J. Mandhar, Commissioner of the Presidency Division, gave his opinion that the great majority of students who pass the Matriculation Examination are incapable of following intelligently lectures given in English and he is satisfied "that the use of English as the medium of instruction and examination in the university course is chiefly responsible for the very low standard of what is called higher education in this country." So convinced an advocate of English as Principal

Paranjpe admits that 'it is necessary to give candidates the option of using vernacular at Matriculation.'

The Indian mind has gradually been awakening to the disastrous results of the present systems of teaching non-language subjects through the medium of English. The question is widely being asked whether the time of energy spent in acquiring a foreign tongue like English, the genius of which is different from ours, not only as a cultural language or commercial *Lingua Franca,* but mastering its grammar in order to try and use it as the vehicle of every day thought and life, is not after all a stupendous waste. As a witness before the Calcutta University Commission says, "Eight years of English school life and three or four years in the college are spent in acquiring this all-important tongue" and how many really acquire a tolerable knowledge of it!

This use of English as the sole medium of instruction in our schools is responsible for two of the most terrible phenomena in our educational world. The enormous number of failures in examinations (especially in the matriculation) is undoubtedly due to the difficulty of answering English. The difficulty that the writer himself experienced, and it was very considerable, in his Matriculation Examination was in understanding the meaning of non-language questions.[1] Questions in arithmetic

[1] An authentic case of how disastrously the difficulty is felt may be given here. A student of history in the Intermediate class who knew his Indian History from original sources, being a good scholar of Persian or Turki failed to obtain a pass in that subject. On enquiry it was found that he had misunderstood all the questions, especially one which asked "what was the military disposition of Babar at Panipat." The answer contained a clear summary of Babar's attainments, ability, &c., the student evidently misunderstanding the word disposition. Herbert Spencer, as early as 1873, remarked about this commenting on the replies given about the meanings of English words in the Calcutta University Matriculation Examination.

"If now, instead of accepting that which is presented to us we look a little below it, that which may strike us is the amazing folly if an examiner who professes to test the fitness of youths for commencing their higher education by seeing how much they know of the technical terms, cant phrases, slang and even extinct slang talked by people of another nation. Instead of the unfitness of boys which is pointed out to us, we may see rather the unfitness of those concerned in education of them."—*The Study of Sociology*, p. 97.

which he could have easily answered, if put in his Vernacular, became absolutely impossible when clothed in a language which was only imperfectly understood. The same was the case in history, geography and all other subjects where the questions are set in English. It really amounts to this; that whatever knowledge you may possess in your subjects your educational career is cut short in the Matriculation class if you cannot understand all the subtleties of an extremely complicated foreign language.

Secondly, these young men who fail in their University examinations, especially Matriculation, have no courses open to them. Their education is absolutely of no practical value to them. They are strained in the voyage of life. This has so universally been the case that failure in the entrance examination has become synonymous in India with failure in life. At present, all over India, the community is burdened with such a large number of these examination-wrecks that it may be said to constitute one of the most serious problems in our national life. It must be remembered that almost all over India the middle classes have adopted an academic ambition which in the words of the Calcutta University Commission is 'an event of great moment in the social history' of the country. The ravages of this system therefore affect not only the richer classes but the agricultural population who, deeming it easier to gain a status by getting their sons into Government Service, send them to English schools. The result is that the great majority of them get left behind either in the matriculation class or somewhere below.

It need hardly be emphasised that India cannot afford this wastage. Indeed no nation however gifted can afford to waste, to deliberately squander, any portion of its intelligence. India at present stands in need of all that she has got. Indeed in educational as in other matters the only sound policy is maximum utilisation and minimum wastage. Anyone who gives the least thought to the subject will agree that our present system results in the very opposite; that the utilisation is not only not maximum but handicapped by so much difficulties that it could never be maximum;

while the wastage is on all hands admitted to be excessive to a degree.

What is the remedy? To my mind it seems that the real solution lies in substituting vernacular for English as the medium of instruction in schools. English, of course, should be taught everywhere as a compulsory subject to those who desire a University course. But otherwise the medium of instruction should be the vernacular of the district. Herein lies the real solution of the problem of secondary education in India.

It is not denied even by those few who advocate English as the medium in secondary schools that non-language subjects could be better taught and would certainly be better understood in the vernaculars. The absurdity of explaining a possibly simple process in arithmetic in English which is understood imperfectly by the teacher and not at all by the students, is obvious and would certainly have been comical had not the practice been the cause of so much national tragedy. The necessity of a foreign medium makes it impossible for the student to understand the subject thoroughly, and entails a great wastage of energy and intelligence spent in trying to master the complexities of so difficult a language as English.

By a substitution of vernaculars for English in schools, not only will students be able to study more thoroughly and understand things better but they will also be able to study more subjects. The writer can remember his being taught episodes from Indian History in the 1st form in his own vernacular and it is almost all the history taught in school that he remembers now. He was again taught the same subject in the second, third and fourth forms, through text books written in vile English. Now it needs no showing that this method of studying one subject first in one language and then for a number of years through another language means a gross wastage of time during the most precious period of one's school-life. The subject could have been studied thoroughly through the vernacular in one-fourth of the time. The loss here lies not merely in intellectual wastage but in the loss of opportunities for the student to study other subjects. A German boy in his secondary school course studies not only history and geography and such other subjects as are taught in Indian schools but others including a certain amount of English and French. If the time of the Indian student could also be utilised to its fullest extent and the vernaculars substituted as the media of instruction, I have no doubt that a more varied, more comprehensive and more useful course could be introduced in the secondary schools.

The great obstacle standing in the way of such a progress is the University. The schools in India seem to exist merely for the purpose of preparing students for the colleges. They seem to have taken that as their proper role. A more fallacious and a more disastrous role it is impossible to imagine. The percentage of students who could afford a college education is very small. The percentage who could profit by it is smaller. The interests of the vast majority whose education stops or ought to stop with the secondary school are sacrificed at the alter of the efficiency of colleges. The students who find it impossible either from lack of funds or from lack of interest to enter a University course are left behind with an education which fits them in nowhere and is of no use to them in any walk of life they may choose.

The first thing therefore to do is to take the secondary schools out of the domination of the University and make them completely independent. It should be rendered possible to receive a thorough and complete course of education, both cultural and materially useful, in the secondary schools. This can easily be done by substituting the vernacular of the province for English as the medium of instruction in the school and this is no such revolutionary demand as some people try to make it out but an ideal formulated by the Court of Directors as early as 1854 and advocated by the Government of India on all possible occasions.

The evils of the present system in killing all originality and making us mere machines for repeating secondhand information have been universally recognised. The poet Rabindra Nath Tagore, who is always pointed out as exemplifying the perfect command of English that an Indian may attain, declared to the Calcutta University Commission his "strong conviction that while English should be skilfully and thoroughly taught as the second language, the chief medium of instruction in schools (and even in colleges up to the stage of the University degree) should be the mother tongue." ([1]) Mr. C. Ramalinga Reddi, the well known Inspector General of Education in Mysore, to whom the state owes its phenomenal progress in education, once told the writer that no great advancement in any line could be expected as long as education continued to be through a foreign language. 'The process of thought' he emphasised ought to be in the language that is most national to the students' mind; otherwise the thinking powers of the mind will remain only partially developed at the very most. ([2]) Another

---

[1] Calcutta University Commission Report, Vol. I, p. 227.

[2] "It is education through the vernaculars that I consider to be the true objective. But they say English is the official language. I know it is. It is doubtless a passport to livelihood; but is it a passport to life? . . . It is nonsense to talk about the impossibility of making vernaculars serve as the media for modern instruction. Where Japanese has succeeded, Aryan and Dravidian languages will not fail unless there is a lamentable lack of honest effort and honest purpose on our part (p. 15. Speeches on University Reform.)

well known educationist, Mr. Syed Ross Masood, Director of Public Instruction, Hyderabad (Deccan), wrote thus to the Calcutta University Commission. "The medium of Instruction both in schools and universities should be the vernacular of the province. Without this our life and mode of thought would become more artificial and superficial than they need be. India will never develop her real genius and intellectual life till it is made possible for the inhabitants of the country to acquire all varieties of knowledge in the language that comes to them most naturally; and this they will never be able to do as long as English is allowed to remain the only language of culture in the land."

Mr. Masood has tried to realise his ideal in the Osmania University started under a charter from His Exalted Highness the Nizam. There the medium of instruction even for research degrees is exclusively Urdu while English is taught as a second language. A large committee of nearly 40 persons have been appointed to translate the necessary books and there is very little doubt that supported by so powerful a Government as that of His Exalted Highness, the movement is bound to be a success. On its success depends a great deal of the failure of Indian Education.

It is time that we realised the perversity of our educational system; that we devised some method to counteract the great intellectual wastage that has resulted from using English as the medium of instruction in our schools. National India must wake up to this problem and on this depends the course of our national evolution.

III

UNIVERSITY REFORM

"I venture to suggest that the real trouble is not over-education but miseducation by which I mean the giving of the wrong kind of Education. Doubtless in early days the necessities of Government Service had a predominant influence in determining the extent and character of the education given in India . . . . . Indian Universities will be judged by two standards, firstly by their contribution to discovery, invention and the expansion of the field of science and art; and secondly by the number and the quality of men whom they send forth filled with a genuine devotion to the good of India..."

—THE MAHARAJAH OF MYSORE,
The Chancellor at the Convocation of the Benares Hindu University.

III

UNIVERSITY REFORM IN INDIA [1]

IN a previous essay an attempt has been made to analyse the causes of the grave educational unrest that has been one of the main characteristics of the 20th century in India. The strength of this movement may to some extent be gauged by the simple enumeration of the many and varied educational experiments undertaken during the last ten years. During that time India has witnessed the foundation of four Universities; those of Benares, Patna, Mysore and Hyderabad. The British Government has itself taken in hand the creation of new Universities at old centres of culture, like Dacca,

[1] This essay was written (while the author was still at Oxford) a year and a half before the report of the Calcutta University Commission was published. He has however allowed it to stand as it was written confining his remarks about the Commission's findings and recommendations to foot notes.

Lucknow, Nagpore and Agra. But apart from the Universities which are either official or have the sanction of officialdom there are also such movements as the National Education Society of Mrs. Besant and the Women's University of Prof. Kharve, which undertake to carry on a task of some magnitude in attempting to create vast educational organisations independent of the patronage and financial support of the Government.

These activities afford conclusive proof that the educational unrest that first expressed itself during the Viceroyalty of Lord Curzon has begun to bear fruit. It is evident that the evils of the present education have been so universally recognised that no one of any weight has been found to defend it. It is now taken for granted that the "orthodox and classical universities" of India, if one may call them so, do not fulfil the function which Universities, all over the world, exist to fulfil. It is also generally recognised that the influence which these Universities have exerted has not been wholly beneficial to society. This is nothing to be surprised about, since the Indian educational system, of which the orthodox Universities are only the inevitable culmination, was transformed in spite of early liberal ideals to a mere machine for the purpose of producing clerks for Government offices.[1]

The Universities of India, after these 70 years which have rolled by since their foundation, still show unmistakable evidence of this underlying idea. They are still mainly examining bodies for declaring the fitness, or otherwise, of a number of students to drive 'goose quills on foolscaps' in the minor grades of Government Service. The system which these bodies have established in India merely serves to divide the community into two main classes on the basis of success or failure in examinations. And the gulf between these two classes is deep and impassable. The brand of inferiority is placed on one who finds it impossible to adapt his mind to examination conditions, a brand as effective as the *fleur de lys* of the French monarchs in outcasting a man from society.

---

[1] For the history of this slow transformation see the essay on vernaculars as the media of instruction.

In fact the "failed B. A. candidate" of our Universities is the Pariah of the modern educational world.

The curricula of the Universities also show the definite object for which they were brought into existence. The most important course of study in the college classes is the English language, an absolute mastery in which seems to have been the be all and end all of your educational life. In fact it was claimed as a supreme distinction, compared to which every other intellectual attainment was a mere nothing, that some people could write English as well as (or is it 'better than') Englishmen. It is an illuminating, if by no means complimentary, comment on the extent of the demoralisation that the Anglo-Indian educational policy has been able to effect that we Indians should have sunk so far down (as we undoubtedly did in the 80's and the 90's) as to consider a comparatively absolute mastery of English the supreme achievement for our intellect.

This was the inevitable result of the excessive importance attached in the curricula of the Universities to the study of English, the reading and writing of which with freedom were absolutely necessary for work under Government. Everything in the University was subordinated to this all important purpose of recruiting for the subordinate grades of Government Service. The study of sciences necessary to equip a man in the struggles of the modern world was neglected; scholarship was relegated to the back ground; Sanskrit and Persian, the two main classic languages of India, found hardly any place in the Universities at all. And more surprising was the omission of such languages as Hindi and Bengali, Tamil and Telugu, from the higher studies of the University.

Another characteristic of our orthodox Universities which still betray the purpose for which they were founded is the place given to the study of subjects relating to India. Till very recently none of the Universities of India had any facilities for work of any sort, elementary or advanced with regard to Indian History. Indian economics were *tabu* as far as the authorities of the Universities were concerned and they even went to the extent of forcing down our throats the absolutely inapplicable principles of a system of national economics which the peculiar conditions of England had given rise to. The University authorities seemed to have completely ignored the very existence of economic phenomena in India, apart of course from the principles of free trade, Imperial Preference and such other things. And, curiously enough, though for the study of sociology[1], India offers a unique and extensive field, and for Anthropology a veritable museum of the highest interest, in neither of these subjects have any of the Indian Universities shown the least interest or for their study the least sympathy.

In fact the Universities of India have made no attempt to adapt themselves to the intellectual needs of the country. They have not-been-seats of learning where the torch of scholarship and culture has been held high for the enlight-

---

Since this was written the Bombay University has instituted a chair for sociology, for which they have secured the services of that eminent thinker Prof. Patrick Geddes. It is certainly a move in the right direction. But when will the authorities recognise that Anthropology is as important?

enment of the people. Nor have they attempted to interpret social ideals and values and help in the great readjustment that is taking place within the Indian society. Our Universities, we can say without qualification, have been the citadels of prejudice against Indian culture.

The main results of the orthodox Universities apart from those resulting from the narrowness of its objective may now be considered. In this connection we should bear in mind that a University exists primarily for three objects. First, it is a place the main activities of which are directed for the purpose of augmenting the world's stock of knowledge, where knowledge is sought for its own sake, and developed and expounded for the good of the world. Secondly, a University is the place to which one looks for the proper aesthetic development of the nation, for the cultivation and refinement of the power of enjoyment. Thirdly, it is a qualifying place for professions, whence the whole body of lawyers, medical men, engineers and the rest of them emerge. In short, the University is a seat of higher research, a centre of liberal culture, and a place for qualifying professional men.

Of these, the last, though a necessary incident, is not an essential characteristic. The strictly utilitarian view which considers a University as a mere board for certifying efficiency in certain professions is one that brings it down from its high estate to the position of a polytechnique. A polytechnique qualifies men for various minor professions, but it is not a university. The Inns of Court qualify those who eat their dinners and pass their examination to practise as Barristers but the Council of Legal Education does not claim to be a University. On the other hand, Oxford which boasts that it does not train the vast majority of its students to any profession is considered the leading University of the Empire and its intellectual capital. Thus a University exists mainly as a centre of culture, for the refinement of the aesthetic enjoyment of a people and for the augmentation of the stock of man's knowledge. Indian Universities fail in all these.

It is unnecessary to examine in detail their failure in these vital matters. They do not profess to be institutions devoted to the search of truth, nor have they claimed till recently that the pursuit of knowledge was among their objects. Research had no place till very recently in the prospectus of any Indian University and even now it is given a very minor place except perhaps in the University of Calcutta. What has been the result? After 70 years of the most strenuous activities none of our universities have been able to say that they have founded a school of thought, or contributed to the growth of any science. The extremely narrow ideal of our Universities had left us with a mere knowledge of English and nothing else. They have forgotten that higher thought and research work are the bases on which national greatness and national prosperity depend. The change from a synnomic to a syntelic state of society, from a state in which an unconscious following of custom is the principle of social life to one in which conscious alterations are made in social structure and society, is led by the higher thoughts and ideals of its enlightened section. This fundamental change, which really marks the evolution of progressive from stationary societies, cannot be carried out where the centres of culture do not give every facility for independent thinking and higher research. Again research in sciences apart from the value it possesses in adding to the world's knowledge is the real basis of material prosperity. Science and practice, in Mr. Balfour's beautiful phrase, have met in fruitful embrace and now it is perfectly impossible that any nation should keep in the van of industrial progress if it ignores or neglects the teachings of science. The results of higher researches are not in these days merely embodied in unintelligible theses but find immediate and practical shape in altering some important process in industry or creating new ones. This wedding of scientific research to industrial progress has been one of the capital facts of the last 50 years in Europe. Yet the only practical realisation of that idea in India came from the generous munificence of the late J. N. Tata. Herein our Universities have shown themselves to be hopelessly behind times and wholly unresponsive to the interests and demands of our country.

Again, our Universities do not claim to exist for the purpose of moulding the taste or augmenting the aesthetic pleasure of the Indian people. It is unnecessary for us to dilate on the very high value of aesthetical training in national life and its greater importance not only as a necessary element of culture but as an instrument of education. With it is entwined the study of humanities which undoubtedly ought to be the basis of every true education. No University education can be complete, no education can be said to have served its purpose, which leaves the student unacquainted with the great literary masterpieces and unfamiliar with at least one of the great classical literatures of the world. A study of Humanities will have that liberalising effect of developing one's finer sensibilities only when it is possible to appreciate their true beauty and enter into their spirit. This is possible only with those languages, dead or living, from which the community derives its intellectual life. For us Indians an intensive study of Greek or Latin would not have the same beneficial effect as a close familiarity with the masterminds of Ancient India. And what have the Universities done in this line? Neither Sanskrit nor Persian finds a prominent place in their curriculum and not one of them has instituted a school of oriental humanities in which the literature and thought of our ancient languages can be thoroughly and critically studied.

If our Universities found that the peculiar conditions of India made it impossible for them to realise these high ideals, they could have undertaken the scarcely less important function of popularising knowledge already gained. But in this also they failed, mainly owing to the narrowness of objective which made University education in India an artificial process for the continued supply of minor officials. The popularisation of education can be done only through the vernaculars. But unfortunately for India, her Universities have never been able to recognise that the "filtration process" on which they set their hopes was bound to fail as long as they made English the sole language of culture and the only medium for higher education in the country. Thus the only ideal which our Universities have been able to realise has been that of mere examining bodies.

A University, it can hardly be denied, is merely prostituting its opportunities for benefitting and influencing a nation if it is content to be a mere examination board. This degradation of purpose is the outstanding fact in the history of our Universities. They had infinite possibilities for doing good, if the right ideal was adopted and the right method pursued. But they shirked it. This failure has cost India a good deal; and the central problem of our educational world now is to create new ideals: to eradicate utterly the ideal of the Universities being mere recruiting boards to the subordinate ranks of government service and to make the Universities an influence in national life in all its aspects.

The first man who really grasped the crux of the problem was an aristocrat of the old type whose fine instincts of perception were neither blunted nor dimmed by 'education' at an Indian university. Sir Syed Ahmad recognised clearly that education was the building up of character and the training of perceptions. He saw where and why the Indian Universities failed. He set himself to the solution of this problem as far as his community was concerned. His attempts were laughed at by the educated leaders of the time. They watched with silent amusement or avowed contempt his quadrangles bigger than those of Trinity at Cambridge or Christ Church at Oxford. But the institution which Sir Syed started to remedy the obvious defects of the current system of Indian University education has prospered to such an extent that his dream, scarcely more than whispered at that time, of an independent Muslim University at Aligarh is now on the point of realisation.

The general awakening which was the indirect result of Lord Curzon's viceroyalty was also visible in educational matters and since 1904 a definite movement for University reform may be said to have been started. The National Council of Education in Bengal, and the Benares Hindu University were the results of this activity. Though the former failed as an educational experiment, its reaction on the Calcutta University was immense and its influence is to be noticed in the fundamental change that has come over the Calcutta University.

The cry of the reformers was for residential Universities. Enamoured of the names of Oxford and Cambridge, they wanted to transplant those institutions to India and nothing else was heard of for a time except the demand for the introduction of the residential system into Indian Universities. What made the demand plausible and the cry popular was the undoubted fact that no attempt was being made by any educational institution to provide accommodation for its students. Upcountry students living in towns had more often than otherwise to shift for themselves in the matter of boarding and lodging without any help from College authorities. The result had been deplorable. The surroundings in which the students lived were insanitary: their food was generally of very poor quality and their private life was absolutely uncontrolled. This state of affairs lent weight to the plea for a 'residential system.'

It is undoubtedly necessary to provide accommodation for students and train them up according to certain ideals and traditions. But whether it is desirable that the "Residential system" of Oxford and Cambridge should be transplanted to India is a point more open to doubt. It may also be questioned whether such transplantation, if it is possible, would be the success that its advocates predict it would be.

It is contented by the ' Reformers ' (and most of them, it should be remembered, have never been at Oxford or Cambridge) that we have only to establish two universities with a number of colleges where students reside with all the luxuries they are supplied with at Oxford or Cambridge, to produce two intellectual centres from which will radiate all the light and heat necessary to carry us forward. In my opinion this view is essentially false. The residential system has none of the merits attributed to it; and the greatness of Oxford and Cambridge has nothing to do with it either. Its reproduction in India is bound to be a hopeless failure, probably disastrous, but certainly costly to the nation.

The following preliminary considerations have to be kept in mind in any discussion of the characteristic features of the residential system.

The system of Oxford and Cambridge is a growth peculiar to those places and it embodies a tradition which it has taken 700 years to build up. It is not met with elsewhere in the world for the obvious reason that it does not suit any other condition. The Oxford system imparts a 'status' education meant more for the purpose of producing a governing class. Its greatness as a centre of culture and a home of higher thought, does not depend upon its residential system but on the encouragement it gives to that small percentage of its students who settle down and work there after their university course. Thus Oxford has two phases, first, the residential system which as a system of education is certainly bad; witness its extremely high cost, the intellectual wastage it involves in a very large percentage of cases and its sectional and exclusive character. But there is the second phase where the brilliant undergraduates bloom out as Fellows of some college, comfortably settled for life with an independent position in the world. It is this body of fellows, tutors, and lecturers, who are merely students paid to study, that keep up the university as an intellectual centre in spite of the obvious evils of the residential system.

If the residential system at Oxford and Cambridge is not an efficient educational system, how is it, it may be asked, that the 'varsities turn out year by year the very best men in the empire, well-bred, honest, with keen sense of honour and duty. It is certainly true that the average university man is trained to serve his community and his country : but does the credit belong to Oxford or Cambridge entirely ? It is to the Public Schools of England rather than to the universities that young Englishmen owe their training. Change the system of English public schools, you will change the type of your "'varsity-man."

Though the residential system is successful at Oxford and Cambridge, it should never be forgotten that, even there, it is only the half, the mere super-structure of a system of which the great Public Schools of Eton, Harrow, Winchester and Rugby form the foundation. If you take the one, leaving the other, you will be taking the shadows without the substance. The cry of our educational reformers for the residential system was therefore based on false ideals and on a mistaken interpretation of the educational system of Oxford and Cambridge.

What then is the true line of reform? No

attempt is made here to put forward any definite scheme which will meet all arguments. Our purpose in this Essay is the more modest but not the less useful one of merely suggesting the main lines of reform. But in this connection there are two important points a clear recognition of which is absolutely essential for those who do not want to shirk the realities of the problem. First. It should never be forgotten that the great majority of students at our universities are there merely for the purpose of getting a "bread ticket", a qualification which will enable them to maintain themselves. A student whose ambition is to be a clerk in some government office studies in the B. A. class because without the degree the clerkship would remain an unrealised vision. This arrangement benefits neither the government departments nor the students. The efficiency of the clerical staff is by no means increased by the mere fact that they had to pass their university examination in History, Mathematics or Chemistry. This certainly does not benefit the student whose desire is to pass from college desks to office desks because the examination he has to pass is unnecessarily stiff and he has to compete with people whose ambition goes higher than his own. In the place of B. A. degree examination, which is at present the minimum qualification for minor appointments, the government ought to institute separate courses where the candidates should be given the training and education which would fit them for their work in government offices. This will necessarily be shorter than a university course; and the arrangement will be of great benefit both to the students and to the government which is so dependent on efficient clerical work.

Secondly we should remember that our educational system will be hopelessly ineffective as long as a foreign language remains the sole medium of instruction. College professors in India have always complained of the inadequate knowledge of English possessed by students which makes it impossible for the former to lecture

---

(1) The central recommendation of the Calcutta University Commission, we should remember, is the separation of the Intermediate course from the university. This would certainly be a reform but it does not go far enough.

intelligibly or for the latter to follow intelligently. The present system gives a certain amount of literary education in English in all the college classes; that is to say, the English language is taught from the first to the final year class in Indian colleges. What this system comes to mean from the point of view of a professor of non-language subjects is that till the senior B. A. class the student is more or less unable to follow a course of lectures thoroughly. (1) Hence the system of dictating notes, "made-easies" (2) &c. This could easily be improved if during the first year of his college course the student is given a thorough literary education. The suggestion is that the work in English which is spread over 4 years now should be concentrated in the first years class, making the intermediate examination a test in

(1) My experience confirms this statement and I have it from foreign professors, quite new to the Indian system, that they also find the real difficulty in this.

(2) I heard the favourite student of a very eminent professor once exclaim "God bless the Bannerjees and Chatterjees for producing these "made-easies" for I am quite unable to follow the lectures in class.

English language and composition alone. This will leave the student three years for the subject which he desires to study and it is contended that this would enable him to work more efficiently at his subject than he does at present. [2]

These reforms, though very important from the point of view of educational efficiency, would not, however, be sufficient to change the ideal or raise the position of our Universities. That would be accomplished only by their transformation into teaching Universities with proper facilities for research. The Calcutta University at least has realised this important fact and it has made a beginning, however small, for establishing teaching professorships. A number of lecturers and assistant professors has been appointed to teach post-graduate students and University chairs have been established, which have been occupied by eminent men like Brajendra Nath Seal and Thibaut, for organising

---

[2] This is merely the extension of the principle that the Madras University has adopted for its Honours courses.

higher studies and research. The munificent donations of Sir Rash Behari Ghose and Sir Taraka Nath Palit show that the Indian public are at last rising up to their responsibilities.

Research work is one of the main functions of a University. In the post-graduate course the teacher and the student become co-workers in the same field. The student profits by the experience of his teacher; and the teacher benefits, not a little, by the fresh outlook, greater activity and undamped enthusiasm of the younger man. Also, the student is once for all free from the thralls of examination. In India it is examination that is almighty and the main idea of the student is to pick up merely those facts in his books which the examiner is likely to ask. (1) The aim of the teacher also is to guess the questions that the

---

1 The Calcutta University Commission has collected evidence to prove this point. To the question "Is teaching unduly subordinated to examination" 169 answered in the affirmative and 30 in the negative. As Dr. Tej Bahadur Sapru has said, "the bane of University Education in India is and has been that both the professor and the student have made a fetish of examination".

examiner is likely to set (unless he happens to be an examiner himself) with a view to eliminate the unnecessary element from his lectures. This deplorable state of affairs which so limits the intellectual activities of Indian students ceases to have any great effect when once he leaves his degree examination behind.

The other main object of education, the augmentation of aesthetic pleasure, is possible only by the popularisation of a course of studies which would familiarise the students with the great imaginative literature in one or two of the main classical languages. Classical languages have this advantage over modern studies, that in them we could look at civilisations as a whole, can study the rise, development and decay of their literature, art and history. The objection that those languages are 'dead' and consequently of no possible use to us is spurious. The fact that they are 'dead' makes it possible for us to have a clear and connected view of the whole from a sufficient distance and in correct perspective. The old adage that you can't call a man happy until he is dead is true not only with men but with institutions and civilisations. It is not possible for us to review and estimate correctly the powers that interact the forces that play, and the factors that enter into modern and living institutions. Hence the study of classic languages and, through them, the 'dead' civilisations they stand for and interpret, is not a subject that is less important than the more modern and apparently more useful subjects.

A 'school' of classical humanities is perhaps as vital a necessity for India as higher research in sciences. In that should be included not merely the study of Sanskrit and Persian but also the philosophical and literary tendencies of the developed Indian vernaculars. The thought and literature of modern Europe should also find a place in it, if only for the purpose of comparison. A University can be but a poor centre of culture if it does not familiarise the students with Euripides and Sophocles, Kalidasa and Bhavabhuti, Firdausi and Sadi, Dante Moliere, Hugo, Shakespeare, Goethe and Cervantes, Vidyapathi, Jayadav, Tulsidas and Kamba. A distinct Indian tradition in learning as it existed of old in Nalanda, Taxila,

Benares and Kanchi will revive only in such an atmosphere. Only in such an atmosphere can India flourish as a land of culture. No amount of imported knowledge, no parrot-like repetition of unearned knowledge, no mere assertion of past greatness will make India an effective factor in the world of progress. Thus a classical revival must be the very base of our educational reconstruction.

These, to me, seem to be the true lines along which our Universities should develop. The danger in India at present is that our educational reformers, out of a desire to reproduce here the glories of Oxford and Cambridge, might try to imitate their non-essential characteristics. It has been the purpose of this paper to show not only how futile but how dangerous to our educational future such a course would be. It is time that India should recognise that education is not a thing for amateurs to dabble in. It is the most vital of national problems, where a false step or a wrong turning might spell ruin for the future. It may take years to undo the effects of a single false slip in education. Let those who cry for educational reform without knowing what reform they want, feel for once their responsibility to the nation and think twice before they make up their mind as to what educational future they would like their motherland to have.

IV

THE TRAINING OF CHILDREN

"Oserai-je exposer isi la plus grande la plus important, la plus utile regle de l'education? c'est n'est pas degagner du temps, c'est d'en perdre"

—ROUSSEAU.

(Shall I venture to state here the greatest, the most important and the most useful rule of all education? It is not to gain time but to lose it.)

IV

THE TRAINING OF CHILDREN.

The proper up-bringing of children has exercised the mental powers of some of the greatest thinkers. Strict instructions as to the training that should be given to the Brahmacharis were issued by Manu and other rishis of Ancient India. The Republic of Plato enunciated a theory of education based on a psychological analysis of the child. Comenius, the greatest of modern educators, in his great book "Didactic Magna" and Rousseau, one of the most dynamic names in modern European thought, in his "Emile" both propounded systematic and comprehensive theories of child education. Pestalozzi, Froebel, Herbart and others developed and systematised the ideals and methods of early education. In our own days early education has witnessed a remarkable revolution in Europe through the successful efforts of Madame Montessori. In India, experiments of a highly interesting nature in this all-important field are being carried on with great success by the Poet Rabindra Nath Tagore at Bolepur and by a section of the Arya Samaj at Kangri Hardwar.

It would not be denied that this is a problem on the successful solution of which the very existence of nations as civilised communities depends. The proper upbringing and training children, a sound system of primary and secondary education, the existence of easily accessible centres of culture and intellectual activity, these form the main educational problems of every nation. Of these, the education of the child is the crux of the whole. Apart from the two remarkable experiments alluded to before, child education has been till now grossly neglected in India. We are but slowly awakening to the fundamental fact that the most important period in the development of the human mind is when the child is receiving its first intelligent impressions of the world and is acquiring for himself the fundamentals of knowledge. The training that a child receives during this period remains more or less unalterable and is carried down to the very grave. It may be kept down by a later training. It may even disappear temporarily in a foreign and unsympathetic atmosphere. But it is always there, deep down in the heart and this great fact makes child-training the greatest responsibility for the educationist.

The conditions of child education in India are very peculiar. The problem is complicated by the peculiarities of our social institutions and the artificial character of status relationship that they involve. The fact that India is not self-governing and that her educational ideals are consequently dominated by foreign tradition should also be taken into consideration.

Social institutions all over the world have a most important and very intimate bearing on child education. The family is the first school and perhaps the most important one. We speak of principles imbued with one's mother's milk and apart form questions of heredity and inherited tendencies the phrase implies the essential fact that the fundamentals of morality and knowledge gained at that age persist through life. Everywhere, therefore, the family is the most important of calculable influences, natural gifts apart, which go to make a man. If a child has a healthy home, one in which his body, his mind and his sensibilities get proper food and training, he grows up to be a properly developed man.

It is an obvious truism to say that every educational system should have as its ideal the development in full of the potentialities of each human being. The physical, mental and aesthetic qualities of each individual should be so developed that each generation may benefit by a full use of its powers. Maximum utilisation and minimum wastage ought to be the first principles for our guidance. Child education should therefore give equal importance to physical, intellectual and aesthetic development. Undue emphasis on one at the expense of the other is found to have very serious effects in the long run. Physical development cannot be neglected in favour of intellectual training because the future of the race is dependent on physical vitality. An intellectual education without proper aesthetic training would mean a mind devoid of the imagination and knowledge without culture. Indeed the three are so intertwined that a purely onesided development is impossible and the duty of the educationist consists in the mere adjustment of the right proportion in which these factors should stand to each other.

Whether this ideal is best and most effectively realised by what Rousseau called negative education meaning the "preparation of reason by the exercise of senses" (1) is the great problem in child-training. He called the education positive which tends to form the mind before the age and to give the child the knowledge of the duties of man (2). Everybody is agreed that education should be graduated, progressive and suited to the intellectual faculties of the age of the child. There is also an almost general agreement that premature intellectual training leads merely to pedantry and verbalism. But in the matter of physical and aesthetic training, even Rousseau, the great prophet of 'negative education', does not deny the necessity for devoting attention very early in life. For the culture of the body and imagination a wasted childhood means a wasted life. Men may educate themselves intellectually

---

(1) Lettre a' Ch. de Beaumont.
(2) 'Ibid.'

at a very late period in life but a child neglected physically in his early days very seldom regains the vigour of his body. In the case of imagination and sense-training too, this is equally true. A child brought up in ugly surroundings without either intelligent appreciation or natural enjoyment of the beautiful in nature can never become truly cultured.

It is the most deplorable fact with regard to the up-bringing of the great majority of Indian children that the surroundings in which they live are such as do not give proper chance for physical development. Unwholesome food, insanitary surroundings, lack of proper medical care together no doubt with such pernicious social customs as early marriage render Indian children physically much weaker than children in other civilised countries. It has been calculated that 60 out of the 320 millions of India are too poor to have one full meal a day; a much greater number has to be content with a much lower standard of comfort than the poorest class in Europe can get. This phenomenal poverty has made Indian manhood a matter of contempt for all nations. The physical deterioration of the race operates in a vicious circle, weak men rearing up weak children and weak children growing up weak men. The reform here has to begin at the bottom and the physical training of children in their early youth should be carefully attended to by parents and school authorities.

There are two considerations which should not be ignored in this connection. The Hindu family system, the chief characteristic of which is the joint residence of more than one family (often three or four) in the same house under the chaperonage of a common mother-in-law restricts to a very great extent the free movement of children. Accommodation in an ordinary Hindu home is neither very comfortable nor very convenient. Proper housing is an elementary but essential consideration of physical well-being especially in the case of children and in the case of the vast majority of Indians this is very imperfectly looked after. A study of that rapidly increasing literature on the economic conditions of rural India will disclose this one fact, which seems to be of universal applicability in our country, that Indian houses from the brick-built *kotis* of the well-to-do middle classes down to the mud huts of the poorest Pariah are more of store houses than habitations for human beings. This state of affairs is certainly changing with the rising material standards of the country, but the statement will remain true in a broad sense for many more years to come.

That the growth and training of children should be entirely spontaneous and as little restrictive as possible will be admitted on all hands. But does our present system give them a chance? An ordinary Hindu home contains so many children of different parents that even in well-to-do families proper nursery arrangements do not exist. Their health is not taken particular care of; witness the very high percentage of child mortality in India.

In the school it is the same. Long and uninterrupted periods of premature intellectual work enervate the children. Physical education is grossly neglected and the hours for recreation are few. Nourished on bad and insufficient food, forced to a premature intellectual education, with their bodily development utterly uncared for, both by the parents and by the teachers, Indian school-going children present a most heart-rending sight to all patriotic sons of India. For the first of this, the only remedy lies in a wider diffusion of education among our women. For the second, a thorough reconstruction of our elementary education is necessary. The indivisibility of the three factors, physical aesthetic and intellectual, of education should be recognised not only in theory but in practice and emphasis during the early years should be laid entirely on physical education. "The greatest, the most important, the most useful rule of education, that of losing time instead of saving it"—the great gospel of Rousseau—should find more place in our educational system. Juvenile movements meant for "hardening" children and training them physically, like the Boy Scouts organisation, should find greater encouragement and support of our educationists and public men. And finally the idea should be abandoned once for ever that the great thing in education is a race for time, a crowding of vast information during early years.

The training of imagination has been equally

neglected among Indian children. Our young ones even now grow up in surroundings that are by no means conducive to the growth of a healthy imagination. It is not that Mother India is less beautiful; not that *vasanta* is less bewitching here than elsewhere, not that our flowers are less glorious and our scenery less magnificent. In fact nowhere is landscape more varied, natural beauty more effective, than in India. Nowhere the mountains higher, the snowclad peaks more sublime, the slow running rivers more majestic and the primeval forests more terrible. But unfortunately our children are not brought up to appreciate this. The system of old Indian pilgrimages has become an empty form. The spirit of complete unison with nature which one feels during a tour in the mountains of Switzerland has for us only a very faint echo on a pilgrimage to Hardwar at the foot of the Himalayas, or to Cape Comorin where the waters of two seas mingle. We have lost our artistic sense.

The surroundings of our childhood are not of a kind that develops the imaginative faculty. The walls of our houses are bare except occasionally for the horrible reprints of Ravi Varma's mythological pictures. The magnificent designs that we see on the walls of the Moghul buildings no longer adorn our mansions. Palaces and cottages alike proclaim our lack of artistic sense. The Maharajah of Kapurthala builds a palace in the French style of the Regency. The Nawab of Murshidabad prefers a Louis Seize mansion to one built in the old style. The same is the case with the middle classes. They have so utterly lost their sense of artistic beauty that it is a very rare thing to see a beautiful Indian house furnished in an artistic manner.

Children growing up in these surroundings can hardly be expected to show any very great development of the artistic sense in later life. We must remember that a beautiful house is a necessity, not a luxury. The idea that gardens, flowers, pictures, in fact all things that appeal to one's imagination, are luxuries that only the rich need bother about is a dangerous fallacy. It is quite true that poor people cannot afford to have an ornamental garden or a collection of pictures. Then it becomes the duty of the community to lay out public gardens, to collect works of art in galleries and museums, to erect public buildings with an eye not only to material utility but aesthetic beauty. The Mogul Emperors who built beautiful palaces, who laid out gardens in their chief cities, who made Chandni Chowk of those days a wonder, and raised "dreams in marble" to the memory of their queens were not merely revelling in personal glory and "pagan pomp."

But in India those days are gone. Our children have no galleries to visit and study, no public gardens except in big towns, no modern building which expresses an idea or exemplifies an original style. Even our temples and mosques which have been for so long a time the main field of artistic expression have become mere copies of old designs. This decay of artistic sense has begun to tell terribly on the proper development of our genius. One of the main ideals to be kept constantly in mind in the reform of our educational policy is the necessity of recovering this lost sense of aesthetic enjoyment.

Aesthetic education can only begin at home. It is during the days of childhood that the mind grasps essential differences more easily. If the home in which the child grows up is full of beautiful things, suggestive of beautiful thought, the eye and the mind get accustomed to them and feel repulsion at ugly and unedifying objects. The value of music, "of all arts the most inspiring and divine and the most synthetic and most evolutionary", in the development of emotional and imaginative faculties should be recognised and care must be taken for training the ear to musical masterpieces. The ideal of Indian boyhood, let us not forget, is the Eternal Child with the flute. The image most popular to the mind of the great majority of India's population is *Muralidhara Gopala*; the Cowherd with the flute. Children must regain that ideal and let it be remembered that it is the special power of music "to arouse to discipline and to express deep feeling and vital emotion."(1)

It is this lack of aesthetic training that should account for the deplorably small percentage of

---

(1) Prof. Patrick Geddes "on a university for Central India."

people who really benefit by our educational system. The narrowness of outlook, the meanness of ordinary ambition, the absence of fellow feeling, these characteristics that mark out the so-called educated community in India, are due to the continued neglect of this important side of education and of the unnecessary emphasis placed on the training of intelligence. An educated sense of beauty, a regulated faculty of imagination, these are the most disinterested forms of culture in man and they are the best guarantee of the greatness of his soul and the generosity of his impulses.

The training of intelligence is what generally goes by the name of education. The system to which one is subjected at school is mainly, if not entirely, devoted to it. The courses in our educational institutions, for children, boys, or youngmen, are avowedly meant for such a purpose. Education has come to mean for the ordinary man ability to remember a few things or at the most to discourse consistently on a topic. Even among those who pose as leaders of thought, the value of a man has come to be measured, in the words of Le Bon, by the quantity of things he is able to repeat. [1] The extent of one's instruction has become the measure of one's intelligence.

This tendency, though universal, is especially emphasised in India. Here education and instruction have become synonymous, owing to the fact that the medium used is not the mother tongue. Hence the process has become mechanical and education has not been for us the realisation of fundamental values and the recognition of universal principles. It has been merely an accumulation of facts which are treated merely as such without any reference to living conditions. The principles which are studied and of which one reads in text books are considered different to those which are implied in social institutions.

---

[1] Here we may note that Rabindra Nath Tagore in his Bholpur school has given this point a great deal of attention, "Education should aim at developing the characteristic gifts of the people especially its love of recited poetry and of the spoken tale, its talent for music......its powers of imagination, its quickness of emotional response ......He makes full educational use of music and dramatic representation." Cal. Univ. Com. Rep. Vol I. P. 227.

In fact, conviction and knowledge have remained different in the English-educated Indian mind. This is the result of a premature training of intelligence without the co-ordinate development of body and imagination.

The grand secret of child-education, "that of losing time instead of gaining it," (1) is not recognised in India. It is a temptation everywhere to put the child early to school so that he may become a "boy bachelor" like Wolsey. In India, where the motive of education is government appointment, the temptation is absolutely irresistible. The child is hurried through a course of instruction, carried on mainly through the medium of a foreign language, where his powers of memorising come to be developed at the expense of his understanding, so that he may be matriculated at the minimum age and pass out of the university by the age that an English boy leaves his Public school. Need we be surprised that the results have been so deplorable?

The premature intellectualisation of our child-

(1) Le Bon. psychology de l'education. P. 42.

training, without recognising that in the early years the training of body and imagination is more important, is the main defect that vitiates the whole system of Indian education. We should now recognise that premature "education" is not only useless but thoroughly harmful, that it destroys the understanding and merely develops a plausible verbalism at best and a mere parrot-like memory at worst. We should remember that in child-training an indulgence of our own personal ambition, whim and fancy would be disastrous to the future of the child and detrimental to the community. The interests of the child and the nation ought to be the only factors in deciding the course of instruction and his early training should be entirely negative and meant to keep his instincts and nature free from vice.

The great reform that is required in the training of Indian children is, so to say, a de-intellectualisation of the present system. Education should be integral. The training of all human faculties should be attended to. They are all so intertwined that it is impossible to neglect any one of them without affecting detrimentally the others. A perfect education consists in a just equilibrium of these factors. In child education this is more important because the child itself is not able to express its desires and alter the instruction to its tastes. And no mistake is greater in education than the one which considers the mind of the child as a *tabula rasa*, a clean slate, for the teacher to draw what he pleases. In these days, when inherited tendencies and child psychology are subjects studied and popularised by scientists, such an attitude would have no justification. We should recognise and utilise diversity and our educational ideal ought never to be uniformity of method or standardisation of intelligence. In the case of children especially, each should be *studied* and taught as a separate unit. This is where child education differs from school and collegiate course and, unless proper attention is devoted to it, no solution of the educational problem can ever have any permanent value.

APPENDIX I

Extracts from Lord Macaulay's Minute in favour of English education.

"The question before us is simply whether, when it is in our power to teach this language (English), we shall teach languages in which by universal confession there are no books on any subject which deserve to be compared to our own. Whether, when we can teach European science, we shall teach systems which by universal confession, whenever they differ from those of Europe, differ for the worse; and whether, when we can patronize sound philosophy and true history, we shall countenance at the public expense medical doctrines which whould disgrace an English farrier—astronomy which would move laughter in the girls at an English boarding school—history abounding with kings thirty feet high and reigns 30 thousand years long—and geography made up of seas of treacle and seas of butter.

We are not without experience to guide us. History furnishes several analogous cases and they all teach the same lesson. There are in modern times, to go no further, two memorable instances of a great impulse given to the mind of a whole society—of prejudice overthrown–of knowledge differed–of taste purified—of arts and sciences planted in countries which had recently been ignorant and barbarous. What Greek and Latin were to the contemporaries of More and Ascham our tongue is to the people of India. The literature of England is now more valuable than that of classical antiquity. I doubt whether the Sanskrit literature be as valuable as that of our Saxon and Norman progenitors. In some departments in history, for example, I am certain it is much less so " (1)

---

(1) Trevelyn's Life of Macaulay. Ed. 1881-pp.290-292.

APPENDIX II

The Resolution of the Government of Lord W. Bentinck dated 7th March 1835.

" The Governor-General of India in Council is of opinion that the great object of the British Government ought to be the promotion of European literature and science amongst the natives of India and that all the funds appropriated for the purposes of education would be best employed on *English education alone.*

" He directs that no stipend shall be given to any student who may hereafter enter these (Sanskrit and Arabic) Institutions......

" It has come to the knowledge of the Governor-General in Council that a large sum has been expended by the Committee in the printing of Oriental works. His Lordship in Council directs that no portion of the funds shall hereafter be so employed.

"His Lordship in Council directs that all the funds which these reforms will leave at the disposal of the Committee be henceforth employed in imparting to the native population a knowledge of English literature and science through the medium of the English language."